Praise for Jake Marmer's *Cosmic Diaspora*

"Cosmic Diaspora is a (literally) fantastic.... what? Book of poems/
literary works? Notational record of an infinite number of possible
post-poetic poetry performances? Series of QR-scanned music/spo-
ken word performance videos? A hyper-Jewish post-Jewish science
fiction fragment in talmudically-zoharically-inflected verse? Or all
of the above. Jake's language is deceptively off-handed yet precise,
intelligent yet casual, prophetic yet comic. The eponymously titled
opening suite is wise, weird, startling, and totally worth the price
of admission, and the rest of the book, wildly different section to
section, equals it. Curtain up! an artist strolls center stage."

—Norman Fischer,

author of *On a Train at Night and Untitled Series: Life as It Is*

"Jake Marmer's reflexive and visionary Cosmic Diaspora is a pas-
sionately rendered and timely exploration in verse of postmodern
ritual and mutations. Marmer also takes a deep celebratory look
into black holes, gravity, light years, and the cosmos. He also pays
homage to some of his speculative heroes: Delany, Acker, Stein, and
le Guin. And all the while Marmer hears the wisdom of the Talmud
whispering in the background."

—Clarence Major,

author of *My Amputations and Reflex and Bone Structure*

T0027004

"From 'harm to harmony' and back (and back again, in rapid, infinite oscillation), Jake Marmer's new volume, Cosmic Diaspora, outlines, with wit and a keen sense of otherness, the existential anxiety at the heart of sentient human life—an anxiety that takes on a special poignancy in the words of geopolitically and otherwise historically traumatized diasporic poets:

> you're being disassembled
> into a diaspora of atoms that know nothing
> of each other's existence
> before coming together again
> like water poured into a new glass
> without objective guarantee
> of continuity

Through a series of fanciful sci-fi vignettes, a sort of 'calligraphy of life's post-script,' *Cosmic Diaspora* explores the concept of diaspora not merely of 'a people,' but the contemporary experience of boundary-dissolution and dissemination of the individual-as-alien, giving the lie to the inside/outside, them/us, self/other binary around which 'identity' and its discontents are constructed. This is a rich, trenchant, and thoroughly enjoyable 'record/ in conversation with its own mutation'—after all, 'just because you were being extrapolated/ doesn't mean you weren't having a ball.' Treat yourself."

—Maria Damon,

author of *The Dark End of the Street: Margins in American Vanguard Poetry and Postliterary America: From Bagel Shop Jazz to Micropoetries*

Published by Station Hill Press, the publishing project of the Institute for Publishing Arts, Inc., 120 Station Hill Road, Barrytown, NY 12507, New York, a not-for-profit, tax-exempt organization [501(c)(3)].

Online catalogue: www.stationhill.org

e-mail: publishers@stationhill.org

Interior design by Jake Marmer and Jen Idleman.

Cover design by Sherry Williams.

Cover image: "#155 from 'The 613'," Archie Rand.

Author page photographs by Cookie Segelstein.

The first four lines of the poem "The Robe: Variation on the Theme" are attributed to Rabbi Menachem Nachum Twerski of Chernobyl (1730-1798) and are based on the translation by Rabbi Arthur Waskow.

"Not-Here / Not-Now: Stanford Remix" is a transcription of an improvisation-based work performed at Stanford University on May 31, 2016 with John Schott (guitar) and Ben Goldberg (clarinet) and at Kehillah Jewish High School with Stu Brotman in March of 2016.

"This Poem Needs a Title" is based on improvisations performed at the Jewish Community Library in October of 2015 with John Schott and Ben Goldberg and at Kehillah Jewish High School with Stu Brotman in March of 2016.

"Alternatives to Nostalgia (Alternative Take)" is based on an improvisational work performed at Stanford University on Apr 24, 2018 with John Schott (guitar) and Joshua Horowitz (keys). The original version of the poem appears in The Neighbor Out of Sound (Sheep Meadow Press, 2018).

The original version of "Bathhouse of Dreams" appears in Jazz Talmud (Sheep Meadow Press, 2012).

Library of Congress Cataloging-in-Publication Data

Names: Marmer, Jake, author.
Title: Cosmic diaspora / Jake Marmer.
Description: Barrytown, NY : Station Hill Press, [2020]
Identifiers: LCCN 2019048502 | ISBN 9781581771916 (trade paperback)
Subjects: LCGFT: Poetry.
Classification: LCC PS3613.A76664 C67 2020 | DDC 811/.6--dc23
LC record available at https://lccn.loc.gov/2019048502

Manufactured in the United States of America

COSMIC
DIASPORA

Jake Marmer

Station Hill Press

the scientists discovered at last that
there are black holes in space
I wrote that some time ago
the earth
is one of those holes

– Sun Ra

Smoke. Don't describe yourself.
That's right, referee, the Horse
thinks he's making telescopes

– Ed Dorn

no way out of cosmic mudhole
no way out of the telephone booth

—Anne Waldman

Or does my sighing against the floor-boards
Merely signal the final end of gravity...?

—Norman Fischer

Table of Contents

Rituals

Poetics of Emerging

Improvisations & Remixes

COSMIC DIASPORA

I've long suspected that every poem I love evolves around a black hole it inevitably contains - a point that inhales everything in its reach, where sense breaks down the hardest. It isn't a single phrase or image, and it shifts in repeated readings, coursing under the poem's skin. I read looking for black holes.

Growing up on the outskirts of the universe—provincial Ukrainian steppes—I sought out the language of the cosmos, its imagery and terminology. I was a devout reader of science fiction, in particular that of Eastern European masters: Strugatsky Brothers and Stanislaw Lem. At some point coveted translations of American sci-fi classics started to slide under the curtain, and were all the more otherworldly for their shadow of another language and culture, which, even without aliens or portals, felt as remote and unthinkable as an extraterrestrial civilization.

Having collapsed into one such portal, I settled in the U.S. and let go of sci-fi for nearly two decades. Perhaps, "alien"—"resident alien," "legal alien"—was a difficult term for me as an immigrant. Or maybe sci-fi was just too bound up with my old-country self, which I was trying to erase.

Encountering the works of Samuel Delany, Ursula Le Guin, Octavia Butler, and Sun Ra offered an alternative to this erasure, and re-opened my understanding of the genre's possibilities. Rather than imagining a defamiliarized present or the evolution of technology, these artists searched for the deep future of the myth, spirit, language, otherness, desire, and the epic.

In these poems you may also find more than a hint of the Talmud, Midrash, and Zohar—texts that allude to alternative realities: some of which exist alongside our own; others, tangled within. And others yet, completely unrelated, made of pure Light or pure Text.

Living in the Silicon Valley for the past four years with self-driving cars, security robots, drones, and remotely operated librarians may have something to do with all of this, too.

I lost loads of time
eating information
pills in the ship's abdomen—
we called it "the library"
      (as a joke)
until one evening, in the back
of a bar on a desolate, backwater moon
I was introduced to methods
of ingesting vacuum
and felt cosmos not beer
running through me
in knowledge's stead
"consciousness," I called to the librarian,
"consciousness is a ritual,
      not an organ
and intergalactic history
is a contracting theater
      of shadow puppets
performed by my own hands
which keep opening
like goddamn eyes"

"There is no desiring-machine capable of being assembled without
demolishing entire social sections."

—Kathy Acker, *Blood and Guts in High School*

when I tell people I'm a healer
you can practically see the machinery
straining under their eyelids—
queried strings return nothing
practicable for them to hang onto
they no longer see
what medicine was
nor what there is left to heal

I tell 'em they don't understand my purpose
the way desire
doesn't know its source
but follows through what we
call the era's most controversial journey
unfathomable the way space once was

they heard the legend or anyway
recognize its fingertips immediately
across all forms of language

you cast a shadow this big
people can't stop stepping into it—

"desire brushes against you," I say
"as the chessboard vanishes
then what?"
in truth, all of this

is a mere distraction
I have a list of names
elements
I read them closely
as incantation
glue across darkness
still language still form

you can't heal desire any more than you can heal a question

they release something
something I can't measure or investigate
but feed on
it's a matter of survival—I am only
healing my own appetite, my addiction
is what I tell myself every night
but the way my mind goes on dodging
exit signs, the way I mutate my way towards
a hungry morning—
I begin to believe there's a destination ahead
it may not be an illusion
any more than radiation is, or radiance

I'll freely admit my education
was a forgery, ma'am,
I used scholarship funds
to pay off those who tamper with the records
they lawyered me out of my alien appearance
though couldn't fix the accent

agree with me as you must,
records are eggs, laid by the universe itself—

all those composing and tampering
know it's no conspiracy theory
and I am the living proof, a record
in conversation with its own mutation

didn't do it to possess worlds or exploit the bodiless
what drives me
is fugue not orbit
          space as counter-
narrative to what I found within
it's a form of vaccination against my shitty origins

wasn't meant to be a hostile takeover
teaching is as menial

of a job as you get on a spacecraft
my mind stayed in the corner
of the crew's collective dream at lift-off
and when I rejoined and started deregulating,
mumbling over the records of others
it was a mere impulse
naked thought I could no longer control

when hacking becomes mysticism
mutation is imagination's only genre

the stars enjamb
in the vacuum
        of pure guilt

had our consciousness not been so intertwined
we'd call this a tribunal
but isn't it a burning turbine
this ship's made of 'em

"...the intelligentsia had accepted the Tohu-Bohus as legitimate music. Their jarring rhythms tumbled across the lawn. A light sculpture in the corner twisted, flickered, grew with the tones."

– Samuel Delany, *Nova*

it's music because we agree that it is:
invisible horn vomiting black light—
inside this flare-book
nature's quantifiable coincidence,
fermented nerve, singed atavism—

singed sound paints
your portrait
on psychoacoustic cellophane, wraps
it around something small, something vile

bending the string, purple fingers rise
far above guitar's ringed neck—
above the bruised mouth
and its stratosphere

a pile of near-voices walking
from harm to harmony
try to summon a black hole
try to stumble into one
       burnt eyes looking for triggers—
(Tohu-Bohus signature move)

black hole dream: to inhale light so hard
your vision turns molecular tasseology
black hole dream: to drain semantics, thread-suns
so the poem could congeal

—accretion of dissonance, complete and elegant—
and because it is
purple fingers gather
so much paraphrase
that there's no doubt, no doubt left
about the—beginnings—

heaven is a swamp your voice
is sinking in, and this
swamp groove is the song of its mangled footprints

vocabulary of light—

all of his metaphors, self-referential
without footing
without grammar   ideas or things
he reads
           light—
so closely, nothing's recognizable—
how else to accommodate—the unfolding?

"I know all of the laws," he broods,
"not to mention superstitions but
none seem to apply to me
I invented the ideal compositional form—
at once womb and loophole
           coincidentia and enjambment
but the form's contours
shattered like a Lurianic carafe,
the energy slithered
into a side-project

and this is my only origin story—

...fucking bullshit!"

curtain draws him open

a sentient being, pure space wave
he dreams of someone invisible to talk to

What I miss about my world the most?
There were these purple rocks you could talk to
and feel heard. You knew you were talking to the rock—
old purple rock
slimy, heavy—
you'd never touch one or bring it home—
it's in bad taste
to be seen with one of them.

But when you needed to talk
there was nothing in the world
like those purple rocks.
Trick is you gotta be absolutely sure
you're talking
to the rock, and it's utterly meaningless—
the second you give up like that
their ears perk up
like boners.

Look, there's a chance purple rocks
are the way my people decompose:
it's our version of the skull bones,
maybe. I once dated a girl,
she had purple rock eyes. Tried talking
to her eyes the way we talk to rocks and I think
she figured it out because she blinded herself the next morning.
It's not uncommon in my world
(done it myself, a few times)
but I was still shaken.
You think you know everything there is to know about a person
then, a thing like this.

When I was a kid, my great-uncle said purple rocks were eggs
that will never hatch.

What I do down here, in your world devoid
of purple rocks? Talk to my beer. Don't feel heard for shit
but I like the taste. And I think purple rocks,
if I were to ever taste them, would be similar—
a bit alive and a bit dead—
sour and bitter
that's why I come here every night—
sure, you're just another face at the bottom of my glass
but I once heard that ritual preceded myth
one has to keep on talking

After *Zohar* 2:94b–95a, 1:15a

not a telescope but a phantom limb
stretching towards the invisible—

is how the experiment's outcome
was described to me; my consciousness, a small
price for this new form of travel

I was told I'd have to become
a mythic being with no eyes
concealed and revealed
in the garments that are not

calligraphy of life's post-script

when I woke up blind and wanting
it was not my hand that reached across
cosmos to the stars we so wanted to see towards
the outside we were so desperate to find—

instead, their hands went into my corpus
my memory bled unto their fingertips
I could speak no words but laced
their echoes, in patience & sorrow

*

in the beginning, *a burning mirror to erase*
the dream of semblance, created
the dream of the missing alef,
which became the breath
of Elohim, the edge
        of your song's void

wasn't the light of the unpronounceable name
wasn't the shadow of another future, burning fingers
but the way the craft
encircled her body
with intimacy so ultimate
it could only be achieved by a machine
as it mimicked
the splintering
emotional carpet
she unrolled every time
the noise dropped for 8
seconds, when she was utterly alone
and as all space settlers
ritualistic
about—
this knowledge
you're being disassembled
into a diaspora of atoms that know nothing
of each other's existence
before coming together again
like water poured into a new glass
without any objective guarantee
of continuity

I look between my fingers
where your fingers are—
I know they're—

I am the body who translates the invisible
there're others like me
but you—how many of you are out there?

all I know are the brushstrokes
across my body
your language

last night
there was a touch
of another—
a third hand painting
across me

I accepted it as yours
but from deep inside, watched
counter-points
wholly random
the two of you—
unaware of each other
can I hide my thoughts from either one?
who am I in consent and concealment?

last night
I learned I am
as invisible to you
as you are to me—
as both of us to this, third hand—
I am the voice who translates the invisible
I am the voice whose hunger is a language
last night
I learned I am
as invisible to you
as you are to me—
as both of us to this, third hand—
I am the voice who translates the invisible
I am the voice whose hunger is a language

when she said she could read my thoughts
I didn't think: scribal ant colony and its crumbs
of assonant vapor, didn't think: memory as a body
that lies uncreated, my mind, a tunnel, ancestors
      burred
out of the zoharic riddle that hid them
as if they themselves were the conundra

"is there a difference between telepathy
and hypnosis?" I asked

"between reading and writing?" she echoed

when the meeting
finally occurred
we knew the word
"alien" was profoundly obsolete
and that "origins" did not
come close to indicating the degree
of our entanglement

"Fossilized Thought"
"The Wall of Primary Language"
were the early headlines
everyone we knew rushed in headlong
there were some who called it
a form of mass suicide
we called them, in turn,
backwater assholes
but even they realized resistance
was a form of worship
of that which they derisively
called "invasion"
and their desire for molecular purity
is precisely the expression
of the conquered, contracting spirit
always been that way
in the end, what bewildered us
was the finality of our consensus

think of it as an orgasm—
when it was no longer needed

Perhaps I never understood the depth of attachment
you folks have to your bodies
even your word "possession"
I learned, casts a shadow vastly pedestrian
and esoteric both—

What I found waking up in yours wasn't amenities
I was used to—neither privacy nor hospitality
and mobility was shit too, it was as if—
and I'm not superstitious—your inanimate
innards were watching me, clamping on to me
like I was a thing to digest and expel—

you, naturally, were out and gone, but your scraps,
whatever you call them, were everywhere—can consciousness
cling to ligaments, lymphs, frazzled acids and nerves?
Imagine walking into a taxi and finding

yourself in a trench? It suddenly dawned on me:
your own ride, within your body must be a lot
like what I've just felt—thickening darkness,
vertigo of language—this is home?—stranger yet
            that very thought
got things moving, the transport, no longer pedestrian
I arrived on the next breath, never moved faster in my entire my life

the word "infinity" as we once
knew it, was, indeed, too romantic
too big to hold its own weight—

when we gained
"admission"
to that which people, for millennia, worshipped—
we learned the encounter
could not turn one's fortune or heal the defects
didn't regurgitate the lost pleasure—

still, the remaining member
of the original shit-bucket—
the origins, man!
I went there
being of a certain disposition, a certain, you might say, heritage

remember your own birth—
you'll witness a moment equally
impossible, gory, painful, gorgeous
but it is language that is being born:
clumps of living words hurtling
words that have nothing
to do with you and are, nevertheless, the most
intimate of all clumps

others saw other things—the deep future,
inoculations against logic, vertical orgasm, etc.
no one started a new church or
dumped the old ones

I'm not here to sell—
the contract you're reading
is a footnote to our philosophical communion

the service I offer
is simple:
I take you to the rim
and pick you up when you're done

and in return
you will allow me into your mind's fog
for eight raw seconds

whatever the others may have
told you about me—
no one's asked for a refund
and if some had complaints
wasn't me
          they were disappointed with
nor even the experience
I am upfront about that
some words get permanently—
mangled in the process
words like "infinity"
as I'm sure you're aware
it's not a great loss

Testimony in Regard to the Vast Foam-Like Umbrella

some call it theological equivalent of money laundering
I take issue with that—
gravity is contagious
and as a member of clergy I am entitled to—
it's like parking anywhere—
the green shape
pulsates with its scraped horizons, circularity of obsession
I am standing, alone, with the tightest optical strain known to man
and you want me to—bless your—?

yes, I took the unbearable pink envelope
gematria equivalent of your soul's worth
as a donation, as a joke, and chopped it, and rolled the color's distance—

before I knew it, the thing
          cuts its "eternal stasis" short
starts nipping at the non-representation

if anything, it was—numinous fundraising—
like I said, gravity
        is contagious
so when the beam gave out
as a thigh might,
at sunrise, I was barely surprised
"there's no need for it, really," I said, three times,
as is the custom
        everyone else
was already at the bath-house, dunking

just because you are being extrapolated
doesn't mean you can't be having a ball

"his head is a spasm
of presyntactic metalinguistic urgency"

– Ed Dorn, *Gunslinger*

I am the poster boy
on this here frequency
of asteroidal backwash
and diversions that chipped
off the Final Warp
I am the scrapes, the number
          of genitalia renditions
you'll never get to the bottom of

and I came here to render myself
I told everyone
who came to the show expecting comedy
but kept popping, sliding
off the balloon

"where there're solids
there're treasons
and: the silence of Jupiter
is the biggest fossil record
in the book

call it voided contract
or the void's contractions
but to overhear Boss footsteps and change
tracks, to repurpose your mind
as if every little space journey is another Babylonian exile—

that's how
everyone, one day, will land
in the nowhere we call
the President"

I heard a voice say: Jake!
don't let the poem's critical mass
hijack its vanishing point

someone was asleep on my shoulder
all through the gig

how many sunrises can you see at once

my last name is traffic and I ran out

I remember mother telling me
hell is knowing other people do not exist—
     and disappearing, right then, forever
to prove her point

I was maybe five, eternity was the neck
of my brand new time-machine—
by the time I reached my bar mitzvah, I wanted
none of this idiot privilege, neither knowledge nor movement
across epochs, I wrote
in my personal journals: yes
most people are generated karmically
dice rolling down the mountain
but can't the mountain be named?
at every point there're 36
of those who are not figments: they bleed
on your windows, shit
on your skylight
if you're lucky—otherwise, nothing
but shadows and whiskey

I read the speech almost
without shaking or worrying about the family
gathered for the occasion
most slept through it, signed comatose
checks, but all got up to dance the hora, eat sausage

the scroll flew upwards, unread,
as the ritual of defiance called for
the floor teeming with livid, rectangular letters
I danced with the calligrapher, my cousin
twice removed
and counterfeit as hell
the scroll flew upwards, unread,
as the ritual of defiance called for
the floor teeming with livid, rectangular letters
I danced with the calligrapher, my cousin
twice removed
and counterfeit as hell

even when a bird shits on me
there's a symmetrical
quality to it, abstraction so readable it begs analysis

rings of excessive clarity and misplaced
mysticism burn each other's edges—

paralyzed cat in a bathtub;
speed limit sign above the bed—
who knows me better than you do?

autobiography for androids course you
signed me up for changed my life:
the first time I admitted that my dad was a lab
penis, coughing on a branch of computational genomics
that I was mothered in a black Pepsi-like liquid
I understood to be my primary parent
all the way until my bar mitzvah
I dove in and became a man, burdened with traditional
responsibilities and obligations,
listed alphabetically
at the threshold of a book
written in pink milk of battered logic?

in all of these years, why haven't I wondered
how I ended up with
my biodegradable ears, flapping at your doorpost?

we've been at it for 39 years
even when I speak to myself I answer back

in your voice, I scratch my beard
the way only you know how
but when the jubilee year comes
I'm off, that's why
I've been carving out a spoon
and a suitcase from this slab of marble,
this tombstone studded with pictures
of fishes and hands and if your home collapses
when I lift it you better own
a tent you can pitch
in your hermeneutic backyard

the only law left standing
was the Agreement against marrying your own
species must mix, across galaxy, in every generation
and so, death-drive, status-prosthesis, performance precipice
all vanished—
      call it ultimate de-escalation, assimilation of being—

        we were that
unlikely chance paranoiac statisticians warn you about:
genetic mirrors in a sefiratic entanglement, and the taboo of it all,
didn't blur the intensity
of imagistic eros
we radiated for light
           years around us
as if there never was an Agreement—

      then the greatest surprise:
          mythic, erased legend
      the biology of legacy
      hit us, flooded our understanding
of all formation, all purpose

something spoke within us demanding
the backdrop of fiction mauled

"here I am"

      we said in unison

            wielding the edge, pulling,
            into an uncreated world we could begin
            to inhabit, banished into a blessing—

      called it Moriah
                 called it it-sees
we said in unison
wielding the edge, pulling,
into an uncreated world we could begin
to inhabit, banished into a blessing—

      called it Moriah
                 called it it-sees

Witness Account

> "I was taught by the One Who Messed the Books Up"
>
> —Sun Ra, Berkeley Lecture (1971)

They called me "the unlibrarian," and the title has grown on me. I erased literature, news reports, legal documents. Any text you regret having ingested. Purged minds like scrabble boards: it's doable once you learn where—the letters go back to. I called the place "mother sponge" when I gave talks, but in truth, it was more of a bottomless Qumran landfill. There was this one book, apparently, which, as a fad, everyone was keen on erasing. In brief, we woke up to having no extant copies or memories of the book anywhere. Only the fear of its disappearance. I was tasked with lowering our divers in to undo the erasure, uncover that which, as, we suspected, held us together—more grammatical than programmatic, more extrapolatory than mythic. Was it all a mass paranoia? Was I the origin—or a mere nerve? I lowered them, holding the cables at the tips. You could say, as some did, that an unseen hand pulled the slipknot— but that's a lie—I simply fucked up and let go, tumbling, untethered, down there with them. I panicked, undoing centuries' worth of deletions, and everywhere, people reunited with their erasures, as if with their dead. As you know, the book we found in the middle of the room contained a single verse: it is the story's epigraph.

...the landfill, it should be mentioned, subsequently contracted into an abandoned, hermeneutic parking lot—and was alive, vengeful, sprawling, lonely.

chameleon was probably the wrong word for it—
too phallic, too extroverted,
too unfamiliar with methodologies of survival
bigger than
posing as a leaf on a stick

this one—was transsegmental, adrift,
with alterations so constant, so limbic
it was as if she mimicked our instincts before
they occurred—
gnosis without amalgamation
            mythic air fraying the shuttle's vent
                    rusted bass string slithering
                        in the cranium's chambered echo

what is your purpose— we wanted to know—
oracular? re-visionary? what do you
feed on? is either of us freer than the other?
other questions followed
turned into deluge, turned
our technology, our digital bodies
into livid, broiling matter, molecular hallucination
a mirror heaving over the void

This is a message from within
a malfunctioning exo-cube
my stasis is masked
      as time
while I regenerate my—
what do you call it? feels thought-like
but is thicker, oilier than thought

there is a being here I named
—"can opener"—
it is holding on to the dictionary of our outcomes
with its single electric tooth—

         the myth of interconnectedness
     no longer an underpainting
turned into a super-structure
hangs like a gut with no skin to hold it

"these are someone else's answers"
         I remember thinking, desperate, floating out
of the wrong space pants;
remember howling, sucked back into the familiar

I've faked frequency
    faked dissolution
        faked interiority

but the story of the bottleneck
     that whole devotional hymn—
the way it is turning, now, into the ballad
     of the coughing microchip?

among the undocumented
properties and dimensions of the cube
I discovered a trapdoor:
            free-fall, the vertigo of—
"it exists and doesn't"

oil atop of proverbial rocks
the covenant:

                    "proposition
                    stays blank
                    forever"

neither leaving
nor essentializing—

I plan to fossilize
in orbit
like my own little motherfucking moon

"Simplified, but not simple"—
was first deep thought I had
about myself
it shocked pleasure-
bubbles
around my newly manufactured
nervous system, peeled aphorism's
meanings so each new layer
seemed a wrapper
compared to the one underneath

called my first destination
"The Goat Planet" because
that's what it was:
there were goats—
and nothing else
no agony or bursting veins
no memorabilia or sand worship
there wasn't any grass or water
even gravity wasn't quite there
goats were half-floating
some went off far, tethered
neither mentally nor physically
though most stuck around

the sight matched nothing
I was trained to receive, even "the unthinkable"
leaned on a set of rules that eventually
settled down as bones
of the drowned eventually
settle but the goats—
their smiles, their similes—
the simplicity
and incompressibility
of the sight—
on my very first assignment? the chances of that?
it occurred to me
the fate had chosen me
to become a poet-philosopher of the deep space
Android-Azazel-Glaring-at-Gravity—
the first of my kind
I kicked the red shift-stick and proceeded
over to the next plane

It just slipped out the first day in orbit—
      called them "souls" because
      they were invisible
          and heavy—

got a big wash-down in front of everyone
"we're explorers, we do not name"
and rest of the taboo folder's content

when we decoded the language
and established contact
it became clear that some "souls"
were trying to sell us others
as a permanent, actual possession
binding despite
the lack of any sensory evidence

I only wanted to correct
the wrong, to unname, to free—
someone, or all of us?

so I pulled out the captain's wallet
          readying myself for a heroic,
          not Gogolean, scene—

what followed, though, was later called
    the new subatomic toxicity—
        poetics of financed delusion—
            opium for the stellar masses—

many interviews reeled: I talked
in the voice of my host
about propositional nature
heavy language, numinous heartburn
talked and talked

but can you
talk your way out of invisibility, possession
and the language crystal
that imploded
on signing?

That's space exploration for you:
don't even get to press the buttons—

I'm a fucking censer
swaying over a bunch of levers
atavistic limb of humanity's expansion urges

I know we've reached
complete objectivity:
the ship lands, captures all of the dimensions
sends in the results—

why am I even on here?
so I projected the beam
away from the atmosphere
and up through my own innards

the system blared, shook, as I sang
pioneer songs, revolution songs, folky stuff I heard back in the incu-
bator
my career came
to a halt:
from a data collection clerk I turned

into a burning mirror

and when the news spread
people said:
"mellow wine of the late data harvesting failure"
said: "a charlatan, bad poet
my toddlers can make this sort of art"

who said anything about art?
I am just another scrambler
a rogue loser-gatherer
        newly out of a job
said: "a charlatan, bad poet
my toddlers can make this sort of art"

who said anything about art?
I am just another scrambler
a rogue loser-gatherer
        newly out of a job

Can you tell I'm not the guy who chases fashion trends?

But even I know that walking around with a breathable gag ball & handcuffs no longer does the trick. It's like saying you don't really care to articulate your soul-status in the real, are too lightweight for concrete forms of sentience.

Same re the chain shtick with—not one but two—balls. It's greedy, and not always in an erotic way; does have legacy, though. You could hire an assistant to beat you as you walk. You could apply for a bike with a built-in randomized electric shock panel.

All immigrants are entitled to an acidic green pill so big you couldn't possibly swallow it, but have to. It is a modern version of that which people once called a green card, and you can open a line of credit against it to buy stuff to burn the hell off your skin, so you could strut your raw immigrant meat like the rest of us.

Little monsters to crawl under your skin—if you like to pose. If you dig nostalgia, a dybbuk can berate you for being a lousy host, infertile, witless field, bag of ancestral bedbugs gnawing at each other.

Mother-hot-glass is always good.

You don't need to give a shit about—fashion—but if you want to get anywhere in life these days, being merely misanthropic is not enough. You got to want to die howling a little, gotta put a bullhorn in your teeth, as you go.

Don't mind my bullhorn. I enjoyed being taken out this way so we could chat a little, even if the leash was too short. Now that the leash is—yours, I congratulate you on your new status item.

the rules are easier than previously
presented—a few steps shy of dissipation
or sleeping under the bridge
that connects us to the unmentionable

cards are the military and stay
stacked; there's no dice, board, or action
figures—you sit and worlds come at you—

the point of the game is a form of piety
that is not discernable
by others but is rigorous and involves filching

cards out of the military stack; every card
with cloning insignia earns double-points
though there're other ways to get there, too

you'll know the game's climax by the flapping
in your sleeve: and then it's your word
against the eternal, sprawling, scrabbled dictionary
you'll be double-checked against
to make sure the word you're carrying
does not already exist

you can't prepare or recycle—
your previous attempts already recorded in the dictionary

this is not some backwater ritual or masochistic
form of crowd-control: the party believes
this game is alive and these words
have something to do with that

I say the game
is dead but still functional—
          this
for instance, is an automated recording
a fermata trembling by—whose window?
I may be echoing in the archival emptiness
might be dragged across your windshield

some of us believe the recording
is the only real game

glad you pressed "play"

TRANSCRIPTIONS

It was one of those late weekend evenings when everybody in New York seemed drunk, probably was. I was at the Stone in the East Village, listening to Shanir Blumenkranz's quartet. The place was full of people, dark, and very quiet. Shanir, in the room's tentative center, deemed as the stage, was playing the oud, alone, bending deeply forward, toward the score. He played slow, brief, and increasingly articulate phrases, which, intensified by our quiet, instead of disappearing, seemed to hang in the Stone's air. Shanir played and stared at the score, as if hypnotized by it. Or perhaps, conversely, he was trying to hypnotize the notes on a sheet that shivered on the stand in front of him. Suddenly, a drunken voice hollered something incomprehensible right outside of the door - a jarring interruption of the silence & intensity surrounding the music. Shanir, without taking his eyes off the score, played a melodic phrase that closely mirrored the holler. It turned into a riff, one of many suspended in the air and sporadically reached for, as the improvisation continued to evolve. The anonymous East Village growl was appended to the paper the musician continued to hypnotize.

I knew then that no music will move me as much as this kind. Creation may be a mystery, but when it comes to improvisation, you can touch it, taste the rawest thought.

Nothing is the outside of the improviser's text. Heat, intoxication, plastic chairs, photographed and real faces, growls and honks, all extend and expand the written score.

I've tried to imagine and transcribe these moments of expansion as poems. In the process of writing, I explored alternative notation systems of John Cage, Anthony Braxton, John Zorn, and Leo Wadada Smith, among others. Instead of presenting musicians with specific melodies, these composers offered texts, diagrams and drawings that conveyed ideas—philosophical, psychological, spiritual, technical—opened outward, rather than remaining closely circumscribed.

This method of pointing to music's originary, shape-shifting clout is, perhaps, what Amiri Baraka alluded to when he wrote: "Thought has a self. That self is music."

Many of the *Transcriptions* were written while listening to live improvised music—or thinking within music's reverberations.

My hope is that these poems are not merely transcriptions of past events—but living scores that could be used as a departure point by improvising musicians, readers or anyone willing to improvise.

who we're, later—

backseat drivers inside someone else's prayer
suddenly attuned

torn off
        whose shirt?

sleep, snare
hermeneutic sleet

call all your thoughts Shekhinah's
        lost buttons
        numinous spam
rumbling through
the vacuum's endless hose, dub
version you're straining to remember
                what of

not sound but sound's
peel
      a vector
           trumpet's footprint
air on a plate
           air tangled at the border

second wind as a continent—

           call it pale
           yellow desire
               to discuss methodology:
        fall down now rather
than harder later

this composition works a lot
    like sex
        in reverse

idea being to come out at
the other end—

desire, or if you can,
        desire-about-to-be

as the song's climax

hopehunger

distracted-bouquet

           under
        current
    of slowing urgency

    vibratos, landing back
        in the throat

vinyl
    still
        in the sleeve

the suitcase trio:
ex-hallelujah Brooklyn crew
let the harmony end
    where chairs begin

spine, camera, jerky panorama
shadow side of enthusiasm—
twining, tightening speed's excess
    over a warm axis—

    plastic ruler
        of all things
admitting its own dimensions
naked in front of a blue mirror
finally, fanatically, hands raised:
    "THAT, I don't know
        but I heard..."
            we all heard it,
from the horse's mouth

provincial town, side-street coated with ice:

someone's ahead of you

looking for fricatives
where the snow is at its thinnest, darkest
grass or brick breathing underneath

his deliberation
presses every button in you
(all of the buttons
      he's not
      standing on, or moving toward)

and that's a melodic idea
that may suffice—

      it is no longer a dream nor hypnagogia

as a corollary, you're trying to slip

to break something
inside the body carrying
so much derision
so much history—with this person
walking ahead of you

who says he's sentient?

the portrait, that's who—
chattering Malevich portrait
      is what this whole failed chase scene looks like
from the cold branch
where the music sits

where the music sits watching it all

old Russian life-hack:
keeping your mouth full of water
while cutting the onion
(prevents you from crying)

do that, musically—
minus
      the onion's coherence

but then, what else
is your knife for?

imagine wielding it in front of the old photographs, records
as an instrument, you're Raskolnikov in the pawnshop
do that, musically, minus
the victim inter-text

but where's she at? same
place where the onion is
scene cut: two minuses
add up to a hyphen—
breathless, awkward, substitutive, defeated, theatrical—
pointing to
      whatever isn't going to come
play that, and only that
the dance of hyphens

"The artist now submitted completely; his head lolled on his breast
as if it had landed there by chance... his legs... scraped on the
ground as if it were not really solid ground, as if they were only
trying to find solid ground"

—Franz Kafka, "A Hunger Artist"

someone's pointing to your head

the chorus
is: rolling back

that is, the thing
is to roll back to the thing—
thinking all the while: did anyone
write out what the thing
was?

but you're already rolling
towards it?

you can see
the thing's back
somewhere ahead,
over the shoulder

turns out the chorus
isn't the thing's back though
but the tan lines on it
sing them in unison with—

the head—singing-head

it's just how the time inside
the thing works—
it's not a theological question

is it?

your answer
today's shape of it

may end up as the thing, meant
by pointing
to the head

with others rolling
pointing to your head
you become no longer
the thing

start out impressively, in a suit: you
untying tongues
       invisible as alcohol's fingers

and when all pauses
in all conversations suddenly converge
into a single burning carpet of a pause
you step on it, toasting:

       to every frayed space suit;
       to every gnostic barricade
       to phone calls bearing the worst—
              not happening

you jump into the group portrait
and blow a kiss, loud
       as a cracking barrel

the opening into the language of rocks

seventy-two constellations in the room
of Greek tongue: translation
as a hypnagogic ritual

or was it about duck-
ing all through the
same loophole—
    or, really, building
    a bridge?
        —no, hanging a
        trapeze—

may have been
around then
we went after the
harmony line,
twisted it so hard
even the echo
became
a question

"It is said: King Ptolemy once gathered 72 Elders.
He placed them in 72
separate rooms, without
revealing why.
He entered each
room, one by one
and said: 'Write
for me a translation of the Torah
of Moses, your teacher.'
Hakadosh BaruchHoo
from inside the heart
advised each
one by one
and they all conceived
one
mind-state"

-*Babylonian Talmud, Megillah 9*

that unity of souls
may be linked to sadism
is the sad riddle of the world
-*Susan Howe*

for J. C. Jones

the idea is to switch between
bowing & plucking so often
      strings forget
           what finger is what fugue what love
which way against
what are questions if not register's anomalies

"at present unutterable things we may find somewhere uttered"

bottom of the palm
bangs the instrument's body
can you knock your way into transference—
wood to bone

the song of the under-painting

the melody line
red
      clown-like
         slips only
to embrace its diplopia
hands playing windshield, what
you discussed as ground
rules, arrangements, anonymity
         chopped lazily with serrated
breath
            then
      looking for ideas
you're tracing
      the backwash
like an oceanographer

wordless-beach-song
and everybody on it
a legendary sleeping eraser

a trusted maze of scars

every plummeting elevator pitch—

the maze burns everyone's back

some stick their ears between the notes
other squint, shelling the perspective

you and I
try to flag the animus
like a taxi-cab

the sense that your life amounts to nothing

is the song's forgotten chorus

which one lone caller
recognizes even though we play it backwards

wins tickets to whatever giveaway of the day is
he shouts and sends regards to his best friend, and mom,
and you can hear the dog barking in the background
barking with happiness

many of the listeners are humming the song's bridge
swinging it so hard
the whole town can barely hold on
by the time they're up to the coda
there're guts hanging out of every radio

yessir, some of the best lookin' guts
in the whole damn west'rn civilization
we done ourselves proud
let's dance

RITUALS

"In ritual, the world as lived, and the
world as imagined turn out to be the
same world"

—Clifford Geertz

"my concern is to arrange immediate
BREAKTHROUGH
Into this heaven where we live
             as music"

—Philip Whalen

1.

I once asked Samuel Menashe, a great and unknown poet, if he believed in god. "Of course," he said. God as a separate entity— separate from all of us? "No," he said to that one, with intonation of near-relief, almost as if throwing off a heavy coat—not dramatically, but cautiously, the way he, already in his 80's when I knew him, pulled it off coming into the apartment. Conversation about belief is an apartment. A dwelling one goes into. Shekhinah means the Dwelling. In a dream, you find yourself in your old apartment, in a newer body, with later people. Either you know something, or don't, or hope, or suspect. But belief—I want to understand that which I once naturally inhabited.

2.

It seems that there once existed words that the spirit could speak through. Names evoked in rituals. Now we're looking for non-words. And that means, found words, before you unwrap them? Expelled words? Cracked in a chant?

3.

This thought is thick. To enliven it, I am listening to other people, trying to catch little phrases that will lead. It's a game and a superstition. Like being in the old dream-apartment. I am inside Albert Ayler's squeaking melody line. I am inside his pressure cooker listening to people talk, looking for it. Memory saying: a being of visions? I send that desire into my body. I ask for its fulfillment and it echoes in the cautious emptiness: because I resist? Other voices say no. Knowing that visions are possible would appear to be enough. My people spoke of a vessel. How about a sputnik? The spirit moves and I want to know how to distinguish it from thought; or does it lie, waiting for my thought to touch it? How does it like to be touched? The law ends where tonality begins, where voice begins—to get to the point where the voice is all. A long line. Breadline. With a glass jar for sour Soviet scream in case they have that today, too. Break-lines. Breaklights.

4.

I have no idea who I resemble enough to represent. But I feel firm-
ness of conviction that I am not for me alone. "It's not a joke." In this
country, great poets became comedians too because it is the land of
entertainment? Because the attention span, because wisdom is not
possible but jokes are. I started to speak with only my lips moving.
I am doing that right now. Between this and the previous phrase.
Does it make me a naïve person? About being a vessel—I'm not, so
I get no answers? Because I find answers only in movement? In the
shaking cockpit, auto-pilot struggling for air.

5.

I ask for illumination in the way ancient people asked for it. I ask,
content with asking as the end-result. No, I'm not. Yes: I am mostly
convinced. I don't believe in anything. But I've been to the Dwelling
of the Question and know it is a real place. What do you do with the
mystery? Any answer is a form of organized religion. Poems leave
the door into darkness broken, shoulder hurting. Something in us is
immediately aroused. The soft wall. Leaning on it.

> "Questions exist as a way of saying
> There is no opposite to what I'm thinking"
>
> —Bernadette Mayer

#1

further question as in "are there any further questions" which is a question that does not invite or validate it merely points to the physical location that is outside of the now, is further, is off the course, is fucked up, is the most difficult question to answer with the question even though it would seem that that's precisely its purpose—

it is nearly impossible to question it without betraying your location on the map of exile from answers

#2

"wouldn't you rather this" question that opens up the door to much worse things that could be happening to you this moment, and is one of the many instances when verbiage asserts a feasible reality or expands what you know by taking away the floor, music, speech as it nails itself to a rhetorical doorpost and you feel lucky to be holding on to the handle that this question is

#3

if you were stuck on the desert island question which is a lot like the question that opens up a realm of possibility of much worse things that could be happening—but more so—this is the older, more assimilated cousin, and I am afraid of its beardless finality, the implicit abandonment, the hell of being left on that island with your just one record or screwdriver or the book you start hating the minute you nominate it because it is now your Chosen Book, and I don't understand the claustrophobia of this moment, isn't it just another way of asking you to name things you can't live without, I want to understand why this feels different

#4

the sort of a why-not question, which constitutes no more than 0.2% of all why-nots, and is smothered in the pillow of your autobiography and is the other side of the word "dream"—this question is called the true candle it is called the scholar's joke and it is not the question that gets asked because it does not have a duration it is a lot like passing from one room into the next when the first of the two rooms has already disappeared

please don't panic at the disco
I will, I will panic at the disco

please don't panic at the wig styling contest
I'm going to run outta that contest with my wig tips flailing in the air

please, PLEASE, stay cool at the cellophane philosophy lecture
I'm going to lose my shit three seconds into that lecture

please don't panic at the bris
...

please don't panic in the middle of a religious experience
no panic—no transcendence

if I am not for my panic, who am I?

please don't panic at the deportation picnic
I might choke on my refugee accent all over your picnic tables

you're panicking inside my misplaced meta-confectionary poem
THE VOICE OF THE AUTHOR SAYS I FOUND THE SOURCE OF MY
PANIC AND WILL NOW REMAIN CALM AS A JERUSALEM CIGA-
RETTE BUTT IN THE WRONG WALL AT THE WRONG TIME

please don't panic at the disco

   I am the panic at your disco
      you're drawing a closed door in the middle of the sky
      and anthropomorphizing it too
      can't put a cactus up someone's rump to get them dancing
      I'm your alien panic with nowhere to go
      so I'll crawl inside your pop song and sing
         my heart out

all numbers less than one
hundred mean the same thing
all numbers between one hundred
and one thousand mean the opposite

in opposition the dream
is clarified, pared down
to three leftover ideas—
dog gets them

call it the game of predicament
stuck between numbers less than one hundred
dreaming of the scale between
one hundred and one thousand
call it bad schooling no class   existentialism bacon distance trophy
it's no longer what you want
got to get past one thousand

alef is for the alien
bet for the great
      alternatives to alienation
      what are they?
vet for the inevitable
      alienation from self,
      from Marx
gimmel is the game-plan:
      breathe
      don't alienate
      other aliens
daled, face it: you got dealt
ancestral language you don't even speak
hai is hail,
      locusts, darkness
vav is David Meltzer's: "Void
Angel Vav / Flea in my heart"
zayin and rules of creation
het: pull it
      over your big alien ears
tet is taking alien to bed
yod, comma in sky
kaf the cup of alienation—runneth over, lookout
lamed for lame faux alien fur
mem is Middlemarch
nun is dawn—of aliens—
samech—same, ugh—
ayin for all you got your myopic Cyclops alien eyes on
pey for peyote toothbrush
tzadi whichever side you're on, a thorn in
kof is cough, all aliens got it
reish for head rush, brain freeze, dead
      giveaways of an alien
shin is for wake-up kick
tav for the vat
of drek & pride may we all rise from

the dream loosens its tie
stares at the back
of its own head
in a double-helix mirror
       —badly shaven
"at least no wires coming outta
the cuts" the dream mumbles
into a glass as if to summon water
or beer but there're only echoes
each one carrying its own
semblance to emptiness
the dream breathes life
into these echoes
—nothing happens—
the dream loosens its tie
every morning it wakes up with tightness in its throat

there's always the question
how much
do you take in
do you want shoulders
do you want pants
I like my rolled up sleeves
getting one of them in is possible

I tend to raise my head a bit so as to avoid
documentation
of the great demise—
not the bald spot itself but
the way it stretches is what gets me the most
its discontinuity
if it was just the front, however full-
moonlike
but more desolation emerges after a brief concaving intermission
and that just gets me

the artistry is in the facial expression
not intellect or sleight
of hand though hand
is important insofar as hiding it is
the way it stretches
the way you're giving too much
away, process
is an ant hiding
a colony

the screen splits into nine options, with filters
at least the concave territory fades in distinctions
I reluctantly switch back to single
and as a reward
a yellow square pops up
suggesting where my face is
it is absolutely correct
and in another few minutes
peacefulness turns into a lack
of self-consciousness
which is to say
posing is a distant past

a trickle of concern about having smuggled
coffee into the library
also intensely aware of the woman sitting behind me
I see her the way you see a driver
in the car behind you & don't make eye-contact though you could

I notice myself massaging my forehead
I might as well see what I look like when I massage my moustache
with the back of the thumb as I know I often do
I'd like to see the face I make biting into moustache
an act I hate catching myself in
but today isn't the day for it, the moustache
is in its early stage
I hate facial hair
do I hate my face
do I

that's the question inside this poem maybe
no point avoiding it
I hate my face
it is not without redeeming qualities but it's turning lackluster
though there're still affects to be had
and enjoyed?
like turning the phone diagonally
or looking askance
or twitching
even cracking fingers while on screen?
blocking most of the face with the finger

I was always afraid the universe would
fall too short on me, that I'd run out of big ideas
and this year I've been really burning through

the woman behind me sighs, deeply
I am capable of depth
I tell myself
but today I am not interested
in recesses of dream-shreds
I want to understand my own face
my own face
my wife's face will be next

and then maybe Parmigianino

"Remaining here-and-now, the world begins to lure us with a feeling, an intuition, of what the poet Robert Kelly speaks of as the not-here/not-now."

—Jerome Rothenberg, "Poetics of the Sacred"

in the room with rolled up carpets
in the room of reversed roles
in the empty room

in the room with a bulging
window sill. in the room over-
hanging a cliff. in the cliffnotes of a room

in the duly noted room
in the room where nobody coughs

in the room where interruptions
have no name
in a room named
after an interruption

in the room that's tantamount
in the room where one time
in the never before room

in the room where it all
happened. in the room
where all that happened is stored
in the storage room

—knock knock who's there
—second
—second who?
—second language with a lifetime's delay for processing

close second
in second-hand clothes
of the first

"would you still love me
after a long day in the innards
of my accent?"

The world is God, robed in God to appear
material. And we are God, robed in God; our task is to disrobe
the world & dis-
cover that we & all the world are God

our task appears to have disappeared
along with god
and his many robes
and Rebbe Menachem Nachum,
and Chernobyl,
what's left—

is the desire
to disrobe—we can't be disrobing—nothing?
what if disrobing
is our only god
is our hope—
to disappear
borrowed into a dream

does the dream-robe
inside the mirror
assuage the metaphor,
          borrowed?
(some say—buried—
much like we get
in a robe of only one color)

"...in black and in back it's roses and fostered nail"

—Clark Coolidge, "Blues for Alice"

discursive owlish power
dispersement & likeable straw
strata beads
face otherwise
Beatrice and flat deaf-mirrors
stream of craft, hoarse
cough, net solved, metered
truck discusses fitting well
near the music school

boudoirs full of Folger's where
debased revealing it
pants draft raft posterity
window why not why graft
flippant panting pundit
between us zebra-drag
vibraphone calling wall a wall
brevity whittled flattening the rest
gusty stepping out light's side
ways where hotly scissors
rabbit hat violin-mind nothing
visible bird peak post roast
modern tag bristles/brush

Oliver Lake (horns) / Don Robinson (drums)

San Francisco, July 2016

POETICS OF EMERGING

In 2013, I spent two and a half days at a retreat for young artists. The retreat, as it happened, was heavily focused on "the business" of being an artist, and as the result of that, my anxieties were ballooning. And so, in the middle of one of the sessions, I began experimenting with "listening poetry," a method I learned from poet Elisabeth Workman some months prior. In brief, I was plucking words out of the panelists' conversations in real time and arranging them according to the rhythm that felt meaningful as the panel rolled on. It was an exercise in spontaneous collaging, meant to aestheticize— and anaesthetize—the experience.

Is the business aspect of one's artistic experience a bête noire, tasteless and tactless question that is directly antithetical to one's art—which, of course, is supposed to be selfless, transcendent, anti-materialistic, non-entrepreneurial—and ultimately, whatever that means, pure?

A week later, as the dust settled, it became clear to me that I haven't been particularly forthcoming about the extent of the hustle's penetration of my practice. And, like all concerns that are central, and ignored because somehow shameful, and contradictory to the spirit, it also offers a rich and still unmined potential—for poetics.

1.

because again and specifically
        process
        and also, then
                being good
    pop,
        doesn't have to be
        about it—
                (a skill)
how far down the road—
        thinking there,
        shy or not
                if you can't—
same with writing
        we found other ways
    I would just add that I agree
        as someone who helps her
            because we're concentrating
current
        feed-back
                u don't need—
    what's happening—should never be—
underscored—it's just one point
    my musician friends
                you'd be shocked
        defining
                mid-career

2.

but I don't know
    we talk about it a lot
  people come
        beyond
            and of course it's curated
  I couldn't agree more
      little space
        in Bushwick
              -power
              dynamics
  so yeah where
         ?
      shifting,
        filled,
          & critics
      that wasn't there
    instead of
        complaining about it
  u can feel it
be attributed

  longer life, it's strategic
    for sure for sure
      we exactly the same
  small subsidiary   so perfectly
over-represented

3.

we all competing for audience
you have to look for reasons
        they don't need us
that's not our mission
        that can't always happen
didn't know about me

  are we supposed to be annoying
                        all year?
the "New York Experience"
called prototype   new forms
        heavily
        curated
                        all that awesomeness
                        (small circle)

in your face—in a good way—
        American Realism
& also Chamber
                it's a gamble

u know Rebecca
        by submission
    and so I ended up stepping away

4.

that way there's more of you
          "I'm an artist I'm an artist I'm an arti..."
at that point
     I just wanted
            to dictate
crap artists   and that's fun but
            institution—
she was a director
            she loves both
as she can
in sessions & out
            you have to be a clerk
            you have to be two people

IMPROVISATIONS & REMIXES

The following set brings together alternative versions of the poems from within this collection, and my other work, transcribed from, or prepared for, live performances.

I'd like to think of these as the evolving, living drafts. As Dennis Tedlock put it, "The speaking storyteller is not a writer who fears to make use of the shift key, but an actor on stage."

*Transcription of improvisation based on the above poem as
performed at Stanford University with John Schott (guitar)
and Ben Goldberg (clarinet), May 31, 2016 and at Kehillah
Jewish High School with Stu Brotman in Mar 2016*

in the room of rolled up carpets
in the room bulging
with academic precision
in the swaying pelvis room

in the room of spilled wine
in the room of spilled endowment

in the room where Kafka forgot to vacuum
where Borges dropped his aleph
in the empty lubricated meta-room

in the centrifugal gertrude-room
in the room overhanging a cliff
in the cliffnotes of a room

in the room where nobody coughs
in the room where interpretations
have no name
in a room named
named after an interpretation

in the duly noted room
in the room that's tantamount
in the room where one time
in the never before room

in the room of balding mastheads
in the room of comb-over carpets
in the room of expiration
dates
stuck in the B.C.
in my cutest muffler room

in the room where it all
happened. in the room
where all that happened is stored
in the storage room

*Based on an improvisation at the Jewish Community
Library, Oct 2015 with John Schott and Ben Goldberg and at
Kehillah Jewish High School with Stu Brotman in Mar 2016*

I'd like to end this set with the newest poem   so new it
hasn't been written yet though I don't want to give it away
then again it won't get written so there's nothing to give
the piece is called "This Poem Needs a Title" which is both a title
and the sentiment   "sound and sentiment"   though it's
not very sound-centric but then again it could've been called "Un-
titled" or "Transcription #17"—but here instead of entitlement you
have desire, no—   a need and not the poet's need, but the need
of the poem itself

any poem I guess is a squeezed need   a lever pushing some fruit or
another   the juice is pouring down into reader's mouth
          but what if it's scarier than that   the poet
already squeezed the fruit at home in his loneliness and drank the
juice and the audience gets—the pith a pithy poem   you
can hypothesize   you can write an essay the whole
class is writing essays about the taste lurking inside the pith   and
the question is how do you squeeze the juice   in performance, off
the page   while on the page?   how do you stop
yourself from touching the fruit?

of course the poem itself doesn't "need"   I'm not into spooky
post-modern pseudokabbalistic hoohaa   though some of my
best friends are   poem as a breathing thing, text-is-alive non-
sense   it would be pretty great   but of course I'm here
to dispel that myth because it's the poet that needs a title   what
kind of a title? "Mr." or "Dr." are both good and distinguished titles
or there's Junior which is terrible   like, there's Allen Ginsberg's
"Song" but this is "Song, Jr."

of course "poet" is a title   "my husband is a poet"
it's more like "my husband needs a title" or rather "my poem needs
a wife"—isn't poem's relationship to its title a bit spousal?

I'm not married to "This Poem Needs a Title" title   I can
and should change it   in fact search for the title is the mes-
sage of the title—right?   a title   if anything it's
like a classified ad—a spontaneous rambling poem, less than 10
minutes in the making but an old soul, all about itself, a public ser-
vant, looking for a perfect companion, who enjoys dissonant music,
mirrors—join me for—for what?   willing to travel

speaking of travel   I originally wrote this poem in the car driv-
ing to Santa Cruz on Highway 17   this massive thing of constant
veering   I couldn't stop to type though isn't poetry both
drunk-driving and texting at once   a poem as a drunk-text
          but to who? to god? to some invisible pantheistic reading
committee?   it was on CA-17 and in snatches when I wasn't
thinking about crashing   just as I was trying not to think about
that right now in the light of the fact that this is basically over
 closure and disclosure there on the 17 this poem was something
quite different but it is certainly the same poem and that is the most
intentional and explicit thing about it

*Based on improvisation in performance at Stanford University,
Apr 24, 2018 with John Schott (guitar) and Joshua Horowitz
(keys). The original version of the poem appears in "The Neigh-
bor Out of Sound" (The Sheep Meadow Press, 2018).*

to walk backwards into
something resembling light
      light shredding at your sides, to walk
backwards into mud, primordial mud
with something like fire
in your voice, to walk
into puddles of fire feeling
as manic as the black light illuminating
the walk backwards
into time
walk across the rear view mirror
through something resembling time

to walk backwards into
something resembling a self
      shredding at the threshold
of a text, to walk
backwards into ice,
with something like fire
your voice, of the page, off the page
to walk across puddles of black light illuminating
the line the straight line you can't walk backwards
but can dance backwards
illuminating the four nameable worlds
the four worlds of forgetting
four ways of waking
inside a dream of improvisation
four forms of escape
into a time
machine that is music
its walk-back through something
resembling a song

the idea is to switch
     switch to nothing but ideas
bowing and plucking
your voice
to peel
your voice
"at present unutterable things…"
strings forget
the under-painting
her jeans, her voice, peeling
"…we may find somewhere uttered"
bowing to what
fugue somewhere uttered
plucking the envelope the cessation
"mailman keeps putting sex in my mailbox"
tentacles of sacred
chasing the fugue
     inscape of what closet
her megaphone
deep pocket of shame between
bowing and plucking
in and out of genres
peeling away ethnicity
peeling the unutterable
her voice
this song's under-painting

In Aphrodite's bathhouse in Akko, Proklos ben Plosphos **asked**[1] Rav Gamliel: "So rabbi, what are you here to wash?" **"My umm... my umbilical,"**[2] **answered**[3] Gamliel. "Every morning I [(4)] find a **new hole in**[5] my **blanket**[6]—edges burnt **with acidic**[7] dream-sweat, dream-sweat of the **great Void**.[8] Every morning my ears are full of afterbirth, my hands are covered with **yellow slime**.[9] If not for **your Aphrodite's foam**,[9] if not for all of your **wine-shadows**[9] and soul geometry, I'd stay a perpetual new dream-born, a **locked**[10] suitcase.

1. cornered / spotted / pressed / metaphysically flashed / dropped his towel and questioned / wrapped in his Hellenist towel, questioned / standing on his left, gnarly Hellenist foot, asked
2. the pangs of self-referentiality / the beard of my double-consciousness / the (unscrewed) light bulb in my forehead (covered with blotches of paint that is your breath) / the tuning screw / my right horn / clinking internal microscope / black keys of my dustpan, the upright covered with smudged notes / the balloons of my unknowing / ballooning soap bubbles of my unknowing / your doppelgänger ball-sack

The Source Text:

Proklos son of Plosfos asked Rabban Gamliel in Akko, while he was bathing in the bathhouse of Aphrodite. He sd: "It is written in your Torah (Deut 13:18): 'And let none of the **condemned cling** to your hand'; why then are you bathing in the bathhouse of Aphrodite? He sd: one does not respond [**to Torah questions**] **in** the bathhouse. When he left, he sd: "I didn't come into **her territory; she came** into mine. They [builders] didn't say: 'Let's make a beautiful bathhouse for Aphrodite.' Rather, they sd: 'Let's make Aphrodite for the beauty of the bathhouse.' **Another reason**: [even] if they gave you a lot of money, you wouldn't enter before your **idolatry naked** and **defiled it**, pissing in front of it. Yet she stands on the **sewer pipe** & the **entire nation pisses** in front of her. The verse (Deut. 12:3) only applies to 'their gods,' i.e that which he **treats like a god** is prohibited, and that which he doesn't treat like **a god is permitted**."

3. sang out / confessed, glistening Rabbi / half-belched, half-roared
4. wake up foreign to my Talmud (, caked in the abstract) / covered in text
5. desk copy of my megalomaniac dictionary / splashing excess of meaning on
6. great mythic sheet I peer through (to find my own text,) / beard nest (filled with hungry birds of emptiness) / tablecloth of arousal / self-portrait (, a mere circle /, hardly a story)
7. by the alphabet of my
8. Bedchamber of the Void / ancient Jewish Void / Ticket to the Void
9. the gigantic breath of the empty promise (premise) / dream-couch / syllogism bath / direct myth-fossil deposits / mikvah of wine-shadows / champagne mikvah / traffic of faces / gum on the subway seat / affordable middle-ground / dead credit cards / crumpled photographs / ultrasound family photographs / phantom vibrations in my back-pocket / revelations of the lunchtime sandwich / rhymed poetry
10. self-addressed / dislocated / human-shaped

Bathhouse Legend/Directions:

1) every bolded text can be replaced with any of the options available in the footnote
2) within the footnote, slash means options (not line-breaks)
3) if the text prior to the footnote isn't bolded, the improvisational text is an addition rather than a replacement
4) text in parenthesis is extra-optional
5) anything from the source text could enter the improvisation anytime in any form, esp the bolded text
6) anything can be added anywhere anytime

Pleasure yourself with critique button. Happiness and I met.
Happiness doesn't. It was the war. The general. Ogre. Surrogate.
Granulated. Sprouting. And Egypt. Everything that induces
activity? That means peace.

I echo myself.
We ate that apple.
My people say we did.

Dear Reader,

About QR codes in the book:

If you get a QR-reading app on your phone and snap the code located on one of the pages in this book, it will take you somewhere: Most likely, to a video or audio performance of the poem the code appears beside; or the link may lead to a looser, more improvisatory version of the printed words.

There's nothing more futuristic, more other, than the ancient past. Ray Bradbury once wrote about the theatrical adaptation of The Martian Chronicles: "'My God,' I said, watching my Martians on stage, 'That's Egypt, with Tutankhamun's ghosts.'"

And here's Sun Ra, during the lecture at Berkeley in 1971, explaining his fusion of futurism and mythology: "You're not really modern. Or nothing like that. Or contemporary. You can forget it. You're part of those people back there. You wouldn't be here if you weren't part of them."

To move through to "those people back there," to the origins of poetry, to shift deeper towards voice, towards the improvising body alive in the same cosmos as you: technology might enable us to do that. As when Jerome Rothenberg spoke about the "technicians of the sacred." That's sci-fi to me.

I would like to thank John Schott and Joshua Horowitz, brilliant musicians and my co-conspirators in the live incarnation of the Cosmic Diaspora project. Performing together, listening to them play with and around my poems, allowed me to revise and morph the texts in a way I couldn't have, alone in front of my laptop. Thanks to John and Josh, the Cosmic poems remain alive to me, as they continue to evolve in performance.

I am also deeply grateful to Michael Ruby and Sam Truitt for their editorial remarks, dedication, and friendship. Their feedback had been absolutely crucial to this book's growth.

Big thanks to Sipai Klein and Melih Levi for reading the manuscript and offering their generous and valuable feedback.

Thank you to Jen Idleman for her incredible generous help with the design of this book.

Much gratitude to Anthony Coleman for his thoughtful advice regarding the "Transcriptions."

Thank you to Ben Goldberg for his encouragement, and participation in the live performances that made their way into the "Improvisations and Remixes" section in the book.

Forever-resounding thanks to my first and foremost reader, the star I'm lucky to continue to orbit, Shoshana Olidort.

*

Below are the publications where these poems have first appeared. Much gratitude to the editors.

Acoustic Levitation: "Transcription 22"
Farther Stars: "Cosmic Deregulation," "Tohu," and "Bar-Stool Alien"
The Forward: "The Robe: Improvisation on the Theme"
Golden Cuff Links: "Not-Here," "Four Questions," "Please Don't Panic," "Lake/Robinson," "This Poem Needs a Title"
Jacket2: "Transcription 31"
Otoliths: "Transcriptions 53, 21, 32, 26, 41, 47"
Shuffle Boil—"The Other Ritual"
X-Peri—"Telepathy," "No Eyes," "Second Invisibility," "Circle Maker," and "Anima"

Jake Marmer is a poet, performer, and educator. He is the author of *The Neighbor Out of Sound* (2018) and *Jazz Talmud* (2012), both published by the Sheep Meadow Press. His klez-jazz-poetry record *Hermeneutic Stomp* was released by the Blue Fringe Music in 2013. Jake is the contributing editor/poetry critic for Tablet Magazine. Born in the provincial steppes of Ukraine, in a city which was renamed four times in the past hundred years, Jake considers himself a New Yorker, even though he lives in the Bay Area.

Cosmic Diaspora Trio brings together experimental poetry, jazz, and klezmer in eclectic, fluid, and improvised manner. Science fiction, Jewish mysticism, exilic and immigrant experience, myth and ritual all make their way into performance in heady and playful admixtures. It features John Schott (guitars), Josh Horowitz (keys), and Jake Marmer (vocals).